GoodBuy, Things!

INPress Self-Help Series

Fan Xi Yu

Published by INPress International, 2023.

While every precaution has been taken in the preparation of this book, the publisher assumes no responsibility for errors or omissions, or for damages resulting from the use of the information contained herein.

GOODBUY, THINGS!

First edition. April 2, 2023.

Copyright © 2023 Fan Xi Yu.

ISBN: 979-8215271704

Written by Fan Xi Yu.

Table of Contents

GoodBuy, Things! | Written By: Fan Xi Yu | Preface 1
Introduction to INPress Self-Help Science.. 3
Part One: Why Our Homes Are Full of Stuffs that We Don't Need | Modern Economics Policies Encourage Spendings, and Over Spending 5
    The Psychology of Advertisment 9
    The Mass Media Decides What is Favorable 13
    Buy Brainlessly, is the Hidden Message in most Advertisment 17
Part Two: Why Consumerism Was The Fuel For Economic Growth | Just How Do We Get To Consumerism? 21
    Keynesianism on Consumer Spending and Public Spending 23
    The Great Depression and The Rise of Keynesian Economics 27
    How Modern Large Corporations Encourage Us to Spend Brainlessly 29
    The Psychology of Pretentious Spending 33
    Consumerism, Materialism is Good for the Economy, But not Good for Us! 35
Part Three: The Negative Psychological Effect of Too Much Materialism | The Battles Between Material Wealth and Spiritual Wealth 39
    Greed and Fear of Materialistic Life 41
Part Four: Think Well Before You Buy Something | Things are Not Expensive. Just Check the Price of Wholesale Market, or Wholesale Websites 43
    Most Price You Pay Are the Costs of Rent, Sales Commisions, and Marketing Expenses 45
Part Five: How and Why to Reorganize Our Homes | Throw away Things We Don't Need 47
    How Our Living Environment Affects Our Spiritual Well-being 49
    Memory Implication of Things and Memories - Wanted or Unwanted Memories 51
    The Perfect Arrangement of Home and Space 53
    Simplicity and Minimalism 55
    Neat and Tidy! 57
Part Six: Do Things Really Make Us Happy? | The True Costs of Luxury Items 59
    Are We Programmed to Release Dopamine When We Spend? 61

Do We Get the Same Dopamine When We Let Go of Useless? 63
Part Seven: The Science of True Happiness | The Physiology of Happiness 65
Chemicals and Brainwave That Gives us Actual Happy Feelings.................. 67
Compare the Hormone Levels: Exercise, Sex, Romance, Buying Things, Throwing Things Away 69
The Purpose of Life 71

To My Family

GoodBuy, Things!
Written By: Fan Xi Yu

Preface

In our modern society, it has become increasingly common for our homes to be filled with material possessions and items of no real use. We cram our living spaces with 'stuff' that not only clutters up but can detract from our spiritual well-being too.

That is the topic of this book and through the pages, I investigate why we are so attached to our material possessions, and how they can, by no means offer us true happiness. Instead of hoarding items, I will offer advice and insight into transforming our homes into tidier, more straightforward and minimalist spaces, and why de-cluttering our lives can help improve our spiritual beings.

By de-cluttering our homes and lives, I will suggest how it can transform our lives and minds, allowing us to shift focus onto the more important matters that life has to offer. The book will also explore the psychological and physiological impact of physical clutter and how by reducing material possessions, we can actually increase our level of happiness.

Homes should serve as a sanctuary and offer not only physical but also spiritual comfort, set in an environment free from unnecessary stuff. Consider this book, a guide on how to achieve that, a chance to learn why getting rid of excess items can help all aspects of one's life.

Introduction to INPress Self-Help Science

Remember, we only got to live once.

There is a need to draw our attention to our spiritual well-being. We spend years in schools to learn about languages we speak, and train our brains in acquiring knowledge for our professional career. We spend our most precious years of youth in training our brains to work for large corporations, how to use our brain to work for someone else, to help the already very rich people to become even richer and happier, to achieve THEIR DREAMS.

Despite of this, our schools and our societies did never teach ourselves how to use our brains correctly to achieve OUR DREAMS and our happiness.

What is missing in the educational system, in my opinion, is the importance of spiritual well-being and mental health of the students. Apart from enriching our brains, it is time for us to learn how to enrich our hearts and souls.

And that is why we start publishing this series called "INPress Self-Help Science".

Let's face it. Our current educational system is no longer enough to support our society's development needs. People born under the new generations seek for meanings in life, and hence several decades onward, I foresee that smart governments will eventually notice the importance of spiritual health and positive thinking in the school curriculums.

Part One: Why Our Homes Are Full of Stuffs that We Don't Need

Modern Economics Policies Encourage Spendings, and Over Spending

Modern economics policies are highly focused on encouraging spending as a way to create more demand for goods and services, stimulate economic growth, and increase employment opportunities. In this essay, we will explore how various economic policies encourage spending and their potential consequences.

The first policy that encourages spending is the monetary policy implemented by central banks. Central banks regulate the money supply in the economy through various tools such as interest rates, reserve requirements, and open market operations. By lowering interest rates, central banks aim to make borrowing cheaper and encourage spending by both individuals and businesses. The logic here is that if credit is more affordable, people will be more likely to take loans to buy big-ticket items like homes and cars, and businesses will be more likely to borrow money to invest in expansion, innovation, and job creation.

Another policy that encourages spending is fiscal policy. Fiscal policy is determined by the government in terms of taxation, public spending, and borrowing. When the government reduces taxes, people tend to have more disposable income, which they can use to purchase goods and services. Similarly, when the government increases public spending, there is more money flowing in the economy, which creates more jobs, increases demand for goods and services, and creates a multiplier effect.

Moreover, subsidies and cash transfers are also beneficial policies that encourage spending. Subsidies are financial assistance is given by the government to the producers, and cash transfers are direct payments given by the government to the population. Both of these policies aim to increase the purchasing power of people, which in turn can boost demand and stimulate the economy. For instance, the government can subsidize the agricultural sector, making food more affordable for everyone. Additionally, direct cash payments to the population can help people meet their basic needs, further increasing their purchasing power.

Lastly, advertising is another powerful tool used to encourage spending. Large corporations heavily invest in marketing campaigns to persuade consumers to buy their products. Through advertising, businesses create a playbook that appeals to the emotions of the consumers in the hope of selling more of their products, thus boosting demand.

However, there are potential consequences of encouraging spending as a central economic policy. Overreliance on spending can lead people into debt, which can adversely affect individual financial stability and economic growth in the long run. An excessive focus on consumption can also lead to resource depletion and damage the environment.

In conclusion, modern economic policies encourage spending as a way to boost economic growth, create employment, and increase demand. These policies range from monetary policy, fiscal policy, subsidies, and cash transfers to advertising. Although the encouragement to spend has its benefits, it should not be overreliance on consuming as too frequent spending can lead to potential downsides.

The government's role is vital in shaping and boosting the economy of any country. The government has various monetary and fiscal policies to stimulate economic growth. However, one question arises that whether the government wants us to overspend to boost the economy or not? The answer to this question is quite complex, and there is no straightforward answer.

It may be true that the government wants us to spend more, mainly because an increase in consumer spending leads to an increase in economic growth. When people overspend their money, it creates a demand for goods and services. The businesses that produce those goods and services, in turn, expand production, hire more employees, and ultimately contribute to economic growth.

The government can influence consumer spending through its fiscal policies. For example, by providing tax rebates, tax reductions or unemployment benefits, the government encourages people to spend more. Thus, in a way, the government wants us to overspend money to support the economy.

However, overspending comes with its drawbacks. Overspending leads to a rise in consumer debt, which has long-term impacts on the economy. People who borrow more than they can afford, default on loans, and eventually get trapped in a Debt cycle. It has long-term consequences not just for individuals, but the economy as a whole. Economic stability is crucial to build a strong foundation for growth, and overspending could lead to economic instability.

Furthermore, overconsumption of goods and services can lead to uncontrolled production, which eventually affects the environment. The government, in its role as a regulator, has to balance between economic growth and environmental protection. Overspending that leads to environmental degradation, poses significant risks not just to the economy, but to society as a whole.

The government wants us to spend, but not at the cost of economic stability and environmental protection. Therefore, the answer to the question whether the government wants us to overspend to boost the economy is not straightforward. The government plays an essential role in balancing the economy's growth and long-term sustainability. Hence, it is necessary for individuals to approach their spending decisions carefully, keeping in mind their financial limitations and the demands of society's development.

The Psychology of Advertisment

In the world of marketing and advertising, the use of psychology to drive us to spend brainlessly has become commonplace. Advertisers use various strategies and techniques to influence our decision-making processes and encourage us to buy their products.

One of the most popular techniques used in advertising is the use of emotional appeals. This technique involves stimulating an emotional response from the viewer or reader in order to encourage them to purchase the product. Advertisers use a range of emotions, such as happiness, excitement, and even fear, to drive consumers to buy their products.

Another technique used in advertising is the use of celebrity endorsements. Advertisers hire famous personalities to endorse and promote their products, knowing that consumers are more likely to trust and listen to their favorite celebrities. This technique capitalizes on the psychological phenomenon of social proof, whereby people are more likely to do something if they see others doing it.

Advertisers also use the technique of scarcity, which involves creating a sense of urgency in the consumer to purchase the product before it runs out or the offer expires. This technique capitalizes on people's innate fear of missing out, which makes them more likely to purchase a product immediately.

Advertising also leverages the concept of priming, which involves exposing consumers to certain stimuli that can influence their subsequent behavior. For instance, advertisements that feature images of luxury goods or exotic travel destinations can prime consumers to associate these products and experiences with positive emotions and improved status.

Furthermore, advertisers use the technique of repetition, which involves repeating the same message or image multiple times to imprint it on the consumer's mind. This technique capitalizes on the psychological phenomenon of familiarity, whereby people are more likely to trust and prefer things that are familiar to them.

The use of psychology to drive us to spend brainlessly in advertising is a well-established practice. Advertisers use various techniques, such as emotional appeals, celebrity endorsements, scarcity, priming, and repetition, to influence our decision-making processes and encourage us to buy their products. It is important for consumers to be aware of these techniques and to critically evaluate advertising messages, rather than blindly succumbing to the manipulative tactics of advertisers.

Consumerism is the idea that our lives are incomplete without the constant pursuit of material possessions. It encourages us to crave for more, spend more, and ultimately contribute to a culture where materialism reigns supreme. In essence, consumerism is about encouraging us to spend brainlessly.

The idea of consumerism is not new; it has been around for centuries. However, it has gained renewed momentum in the last century due to technological advancements, globalization, and a more affluent society. The primary objective of consumerism is to promote consumption and fuel the economy. Through advertising and marketing, we are bombarded with images of happy, satisfied people who have acquired wealth through consumerism. We are told that our happiness and success depend on the latest gadgets, clothes, and cars.

Consumerism is also about creating a culture of disposability. We are encouraged to treat objects as disposable, buying and discarding them quickly. The focus is more on acquiring new things rather than cherishing and utilizing existing ones. This results in an excess of waste production and contributes to environmental degradation.

One significant factor of consumerism is the manipulation of our psychological state. Advertisers and marketers use various techniques to influence our behavior and create a sense of urgency to buy. Scarcity, fear of missing out, and peer pressure are some methods used to push us towards buying. These tactics override our rational thinking, creating a desire to consume without a clear purpose or need.

Consumerism is about creating a sense of identity based on what we own. The products we buy are marketed as status symbols, influencing our perception of ourselves and how we are viewed by others. We are encouraged to believe that we are defined by the things we own, leading to a constant need to keep up with the latest trends, and a fear of losing our status.

Consumerism is not merely about buying and selling; it is about promoting a brainless culture that values the accumulation of material possessions above all else. It encourages us to treat objects as disposable, contributes to environmental degradation, manipulates our psychological state, and creates a sense of identity

GOODBUY, THINGS!

based on what we own. We must be mindful of the harmful effects of consumerism and strive towards a society that values experiences, relationships, and sustainability over material possessions.

The Mass Media Decides What is Favorable

The mass media, which comprise various forms of media such as television, radio, newspapers, magazines, and the internet, is a virtual tool that helps shape people's buying habits. The mass media reaches millions of people daily, and it is widely known that people tend to believe what they see, hear, and read. Therefore, the mass media plays a massive role in influencing what people buy, how they buy it, and how much they are willing to spend on it. This essay will examine how the mass media shapes people's buying habits and the implications that come with it.

One of the primary ways the mass media influences people's buying habits is through advertising. Advertising is a crucial tool that brands use to market and communicate their products to consumers. The aim of advertising is to create and promote a positive image of the product or brand, persuade consumers to buy the product, and increase its sales. Companies invest heavily in advertising, and the mass media plays a significant role in the dissemination of this advertising.

The media also showcases indulgent lifestyles, which influence people's buying behavior. For instance, through shows and advertisements, people are presented with a luxurious and lavish lifestyle that they may not have. Seeing such a lifestyle makes individuals want to buy things that would enable them to replicate this lifestyle. Hence, people are more likely to buy products that seem to fulfill the promises of the lifestyle depicted in the mass media.

Additionally, the media often presents new products as "must-have." They build hype around a new product, generate excitement about it, and ultimately create a desire for consumers to buy it. This is often done through celebrity endorsements or reviews by experts in the field. Once people feel like they are behind the trend or are missing out on something, it becomes more likely that they will purchase the product.

The media also influences people's buying habits through the stories they present as news. Stories about the economy, stock markets, and consumer trends can significantly impact consumer behavior. When the mass media reports positively about the economy, people tend to be more optimistic, and this can stimulate spending.

The mass media plays a massive role in shaping people's buying habits. Advertising, showcasing indulgent lifestyles, creating hype around a new product, and through reporting on economic and consumer trends all have a significant effect on consumer purchasing decisions. It is important to understand how the media affects our perception and relationship with money to maintain financial wellness. It is also crucial for consumers to evaluate their buying habits, understand the influences on their preferences, and decide what purchases are truly necessary.

The media has had a huge impact on our daily lives, including our purchase habits. The media has shaped the perception of our products, brands and services through various media, such as television ads, digital advertising, advertising boards and newspapers. As a result, we are constantly exposed to the media, and it has made a great impact on our purchase habits.

One of the main ways of shaping our purchase habits is through advertising. Ads are common in all media, and their sole purpose is to persuade us to buy a particular product or service. For example, when a company introduces a new product, they use a variety of media platforms to promote it. They would run advertising campaigns throughout social media, television and printed media to reach a target audience.

Ads form our purchase habits, making us believe that we need certain products that we don't even know. Ads often create a sense of urgency within a limited time, discounts, "buy one, get one free" advertising and other methods to make us feel as if we should buy this product now or skip a good deal. Therefore, the more we see these ads, the more we believe that what they are selling is something we should have, which is why we are more likely to buy it.

The media also affects our purchase habits. For example, the news of increasing fuel costs can start a new car shopping phase. Similarly, the tale of a new medical innovation can encourage people to look for new treatments, exercise programs or nutritional supplements. The media can also shape the way we think of certain products, influencing our decision making by presenting various opinions and facts about the product.

Social media also affects our purchase habits through influencers. Participants are people who have considerable tracking on social media platforms such as Instagram, Twitter and Facebook. The brands pay them for confirming their products and persuading their followers to buy them. Participants can be

GOODBUY, THINGS!

very convincing, and their followers often trust their recommendations. So they shape our purchase habits by introducing us to new products and convincing them to buy them.

The media is a powerful force that shapes our perception, thoughts and purchase habits. Advertising, news media and social media platforms contribute to ways to form our purchase habits. Therefore, it is important to remain vigilant and develop critical thinking skills under the various forms of media. We should always evaluate the convincing messages we receive and make our reasoned decisions, not to make blindly.

Mass media plays an important role in the formation of people's opinions and influences their behavior. Whether it's on television, radio, newspapers or internet, the media has the power to disseminate information and form public perception. However, this huge influence can be both positive and negative. In this essay, we will discuss how people are blindly following what the media offers and the social consequences of this phenomenon.

First, the media has a powerful ability to disseminate information and form opinions. Not only can this inform the public on important issues, it can also affect their attitudes and beliefs. For example, when news events are constantly involved in crime and violence, people more believe that these issues are widespread and that their communities are unsafe. Similarly, when the media presents a specific political candidate in a positive or negative, people are more likely to form their opinion according to these reports.

Second, people tend to trust the media because it is often considered a reliable source of information. Many people believe that journalists and journalists are objective and impartial, reporting only the facts. However, this is not always the case. The media is often influenced by external factors such as political pressure and the interests of companies that can harm their objectivity. This, in turn, can have a major influence on public opinion.

Third, the media is designed to raise people's attention and keep them involved. To do this, news events are often based on sensationalism, exaggeration and fear that people can make decisions about rash decisions. For example, when the media reports health intimidation, people may rush to the nearest pharmacy to get medication until they even know if the disease is a real threat. Similarly, when the media reports a natural disaster, people can panic their homes in panic before arriving for emergency services.

Finally, people are blind to what the media offers, as they are often too busy or overwhelmed to do their own research. The media has become so common that it can be difficult to know what information is reliable and what is not. In addition, many people lack knowledge and skills to critically evaluate complex problems. So they rely on the media to provide a simplified version of events.

The media has great power to shape people's opinions and influence their behavior. People tend to blindly follow what the media offers because they trust its authority, lack the time and opportunities to do their research, and are influenced by sensationalism and excessive. However, it is very important that we criticize the information we receive from the media, question its sources and make decisions based on a wider range of sources. In this way, we can ensure that we make well-informed decisions that are the interests of ours and society as a whole.

Buy Brainlessly, is the Hidden Message in most Advertisment

Advertising is a crucial part of the business world, as it helps companies to promote their products and services to the public. Advertisements aim to persuade consumers to purchase a specific product by presenting the benefits and value that it offers. However, the primary message hidden in most advertisements is to buy brainlessly. Advertisers appeal to the emotions and impulses of consumers, rather than their analytical skills, to encourage them to make spontaneous purchases.

The use of bright colors, flashy images, and catchy phrases are some common ways advertisers attract attention to their products. Advertisements often manipulate the emotions of the viewers by using clever slogans or appealing to the audience's feelings. The primary aim of doing so is to influence the consumers to buy products without much thought. These advertisements usually have nothing to do with the actual product being sold, but instead, it's the emotional response that the advertisement produces that is hoped to lead to a purchase.

The buy brainlessly approach is commonly used in the beauty and fashion industry. Advertisements for makeup products or clothing focus on how the products in question will make the consumer look and feel, rather than its actual function. The seller convinces the consumer that they will be more beautiful, attractive, and stylish by using their product without mentioning the benefits they might be getting from the products.

Apart from emotion-based approaches, advertisers also use the subtle technique of repetition to reinforce their message. Advertisers bombard consumers with their messages at every turn, so they are likely to see the same messaging repeatedly, which creates an impression in the consumer's mind over time. Consumers are bombarded with the same message so that they subconsciously gravitate towards that product without a single thought process.

Advertising also promotes the consumption of wasteful products. Advertisements often persuade people to buy luxury cars, expensive jewelry, and other items that have no real value but are costly to own. Such advertisements encourage people to buy unnecessarily and contribute to a culture of mindless consumerism.

Therefore, The hidden message in most advertisements is to buy brainlessly. Advertisements target consumers' emotions and impulses rather than their logical thinking. Advertisers want people to buy in the moment, without thinking about the long-term benefits or consequences. The urge to consume is created by manipulating consumers to buy products without understanding the actual function of the product. It is the consumer's responsibility to be aware of this trap and analyze their purchases before spending money on things that they don't need or in the long run have no real value.

In today's consumerist society, advertisements play a crucial role in influencing a consumer's buying behavior. Advertisements are strategically designed to appeal to the emotional and psychological needs of the audience, and often contain a hidden message that encourages them to buy brainlessly. This message suggests that the audience does not need to think or consider their purchase, as it is a no-brainer to buy the product being advertised.

The hidden message in most advertisements is the promotion of instant gratification. Many advertisements use phrases like "buy now" or "limited time offer" to create a sense of urgency in the audience, pushing them to make impulsive purchases without much consideration. Advertisements often play into our emotions, creating an illusion of happiness and fulfillment that can only be achieved by buying a particular product.

Advertisements also manipulate our psychology by using persuasive tactics such as fear, social acceptance, and desire. Advertisements use fear tactics to convince us that without certain products, our lives are at risk. They use social acceptance to make us believe that we need to conform to societal standards and buy certain products to fit in. They use desire to convince us that we need to have a particular product to fulfill our desires and dreams.

Advertisements often create a false sense of need that is not based on reality. They make us believe that we need a particular product, even if we do not. The hidden message in such advertisements is that we need to keep up with the latest trends and technologies, even if our lives do not necessarily require them. Advertisements make us believe that buying the latest products will enhance our lives, and we will be left out of the loop if we do not.

In summary, the hidden message in most advertisements is to buy brainlessly. Advertisements are designed to appeal to our emotions and psychological needs, encouraging us to make impulsive purchases without much thought or

GOODBUY, THINGS!

consideration. Advertisements create a false sense of need and manipulate our psychology using persuasive tactics such as fear, social acceptance, and desire. Therefore, it is imperative to be conscious of the hidden message in advertisements and make informed decisions before purchasing any product.

Part Two: Why Consumerism Was The Fuel For Economic Growth

Just How Do We Get To Consumerism?

Consumerism is a growing phenomenon in the modern world, and its effects are far-reaching. It has been defined as 'the systematic promotion of the desire to purchase goods and services in ever-greater amounts.' Consumerism has been around since the dawn of commerce, but its prevalence in the modern era has been fueled largely by the development of technology and the growth of global markets.

The rise of consumerism has been largely attributed to the increase in incomes and affluence of individuals and households. As standards of living have risen, so has the demand for goods and services. This has been facilitated by the rise of global capital markets, which have made it easier for individuals to access credit, allowing them to buy more than they could previously.

The spread of consumerism has also been driven by the rise of mass media, which has allowed corporations to target consumers through advertising and other forms of marketing. This has enabled them to create the desire for goods and services, which has driven up demand.

The proliferation of consumerism has had far-reaching effects on society. As individuals and households have become more focused on consumption, they have become increasingly disconnected from the communities in which they live. This has led to a decline in civic engagement, as well as a decrease in the importance placed on social values and community well-being.

Consumerism has been linked to environmental degradation, as the demand for goods and services has led to increased production, leading to an increase in pollution and the depletion of natural resources.

At the same time, consumerism has had some positive effects. The rise of consumerism has helped to spur economic growth, as an increase in demand for goods and services has led to increased production and employment. Additionally, consumerism has helped to expand access to goods and services, which has increased the standard of living for many people around the world.

Ultimately, consumerism is a complex phenomenon with both positive and negative effects. In order to ensure that its benefits outweigh its drawbacks, it is important to ensure that consumerism is practiced in a responsible manner. This means that individuals and households should be mindful of their consumption habits, and should strive to ensure that their actions are in line with the values of their communities.

Keynesianism on Consumer Spending and Public Spending

Keynesianism is an economic theory that emphasizes the importance of government intervention in the management of an economy. Central to this theory is the idea that government spending can be used to stimulate economic growth and prosperity.

One of the key components of Keynesianism is the emphasis on consumer spending. According to this theory, consumer spending is the driving force behind economic growth, as it creates demand for goods and services that businesses then produce in response. In order to promote consumer spending, Keynesian economics suggests that the government should engage in policies that put more money into the pockets of consumers, such as by cutting taxes or increasing social welfare programs.

Another important aspect of Keynesianism is the role of public spending. Keynesian economics holds that the government can stimulate economic growth by increasing its own spending on goods and services. This can create jobs and boost economic activity across the entire economy.

To put these ideas into practice, Keynesian economists typically advocate for a balanced approach to economic management. For example, during times of economic recession, Keynesian economics suggests that the government should increase its spending in order to boost consumer confidence and promote job creation. At the same time, the government should work to balance its budget over time, ensuring that it does not become overly indebted in the long run.

Critics of Keynesian economics have argued that the theory fails to account for the potential negative impacts of government intervention in the economy. For example, some claim that excessive government spending can lead to inflation, making goods and services more expensive for consumers. However, proponents of Keynesian economics argue that such concerns can be addressed through careful management of public spending and the use of targeted policies that address specific economic challenges.

Keynesianism is an economic theory that places significant emphasis on both consumer spending and public spending as drivers of economic growth and prosperity. While this theory has garnered some criticism in recent years, its basic principles continue to be applied by many governments around the world in their efforts to stimulate economic growth and promote prosperity for their citizens.

keynesianism is a macroeconomic theory that advocates the government's intervention for the economy during the economic downturn. This theory came from the works of the famous economist John Maynard Keynes, who believe that the government's intervention into the economy is necessary to relieve the effects of economic downs. One of the basic principles of Keynesanism is the faith in public costs and its ability to promote economic growth.

keynesianists believe that public expenditure can be used as a means of promoting economic activities. During the recession, keynesianists say the government should take up deficit costs by increasing the state costs for critical infrastructure, education and health care. Increased government expenditure in the economy is expected to put more money into the economy, thus promoting the demand for goods and services. As the demand for goods and services increases, companies will produce more, which will eventually increase economic production.

According to Keyinsoanists, society's expenses also have a reproductive impact on the economy. This means that every dollar issued by the Government has a greater impact on the economy than the original spent amount. For example, if the government spends $ 1 billion on infrastructure, infrastructure beneficiaries, such as builders and suppliers, will have more money to spend on other goods and services. These additional costs will also create more jobs and eventually increase economic production.

In addition, keynesianists believe that public expenditure can help address the increasing unemployment rate during the economic downturn. When the government increases its costs, companies are likely to hire more employees to satisfy increased demand. This will create more jobs and, in turn, reduce unemployment. In addition, keynesianists believe that public expenditure could help create new industries, which can lead to further creation of jobs and economic growth.

However, critics of keynesianism say increased public expenditure can increase inflation. When the government spends more money, it can increase the demand for goods and services, which in turn can lead to higher prices. This can eventually lead to inflation that could destroy consumer purchasing power and reduce economic growth.

GOODBUY, THINGS!

Keynensoanists believe in the power of public expenditure as a means of promoting economic growth and solving the impact of economic downturn. Although criticized by theory, faith in public expenses remains central keynesianism. Governments implemented the policy inspired by Government throughout the world during an economic downturn that helped to alleviate the impact of recessions.

The Great Depression and The Rise of Keynesian Economics

The Great Depression, which lasted 1929-1939, was a disastrous period in American history. This reflected the longest and most significant economic downturn ever visible in the Western world. This made a major impact on the US, which has lost a trillion dollars, the stock market collapsed, unemployment rising and widespread poverty. In response to this, economists like John Maynard Keynes began to defend a new economic philosophy: Keynes's economy.

Keynes's economy has meant a change in economic thinking from the classic Essez-Faire model to a more active intervention approach. The main assumption was that the government's intervention and expenses could lead to demand and restore economic growth. Keynes thought that the market economy could sometimes be able to operate efficiently, resulting in constant unemployment and that government intervention was necessary to correct these market failures.

Great depression gave a striking example of the disadvantages of the classic model. In the early 1990s, the US government, headed by President Franklin Mr Roosevelt, has begun to implement Keynesia policies such as increased government expenditure on public works and social well -being programs, and the Federal Reserve Bank has begun to reduce interest rates to encourage investment and consumer costs. This policy actually helped to start the economy by reducing unemployment and restoring economic growth.

One of the main innovations of Keynes economics was the concept of the "demand" economy. This approach argued that consumption and demand were driving forces that determine economic growth, not supply factors such as investment and production. In the Keynesian model, government expenditure could be a powerful means of increasing consumer demand and increasing economic growth.

Another important feature of the Keynesia economy was the idea of the pre connunciation fiscal policy. This political approach encompassed the Government, which increases its expenses during the economic downturn and reduced the cost of economic booms. This would eventually help to stabilize the economy, preventing the boom and bust cycles that were so common in the early 20th century.

Therefore, the Great Depression was a huge shock to the American economy and society. This led to the rise of Keynes economy, which significantly changed economic thinking to a more interventional approach. This approach emphasized the importance of government expenditure not exceeding fiscal policy and demand economy in promoting economic growth and stability. Although he has been criticized over the years, Keynes's economy remains a major influence on economic politics around the world.

How Modern Large Corporations Encourage Us to Spend Brainlessly

The rise of modern large corporations has presented us with countless products and services that are designed to make our lives more convenient and efficient. While there are undoubtedly benefits to this, there is also a darker side to this trend. Modern corporations often encourage us to spend brainlessly, consuming without considering the long-term consequences of our actions. This essay will examine the ways in which modern large corporations encourage this kind of behavior, and the potential consequences of it.

One way in which corporations encourage brainless spending is through aggressive marketing campaigns that appeal to our emotions and desires rather than our rational minds. We see this all the time with advertisements that promise to make us happier, more attractive, or more successful. These ads often use celebrities or models to make us feel like we're missing out on something if we don't buy the product being advertised. They don't give us any real information about the product, its quality, or its value; they simply try to make us feel like we need it.

Another way in which corporations encourage brainless spending is through complex pricing schemes that make it difficult for consumers to compare products and make informed decisions. We see this with things like mobile phone plans, where it's nearly impossible to compare different plans and figure out which one is the best value. Corporations also use things like loyalty programs and special offers to create a false sense of urgency and encourage us to buy things we don't really need.

The consequences of brainless spending are many and varied. For individuals, it can result in financial difficulties and a lack of control over one's own life. For society as a whole, it can result in a culture of consumption that is unsustainable and environmentally damaging. Modern large corporations have a responsibility to consider the long-term consequences of their actions, and to encourage their customers to do the same.

Modern large corporations have a significant influence on our behavior as consumers. While there are benefits to the convenient products and services they offer, there is also a danger that we will become brainless consumers, unable to make rational decisions about our own lives. It's up to us as individuals to be aware of this trend and to take control of our own spending habits, and it's up to corporations to act responsibly and promote a culture of mindful consumption.

Modern large corporations are always looking for ways to make us spend money, but what they really want is for us to spend brainlessly. They want us to make purchases without thinking, without considering why we are buying something, or whether we really need it. This kind of thoughtless spending is what keeps these companies in business, but it is also what contributes to many of the problems we face as a society.

One of the primary ways that modern large corporations try to get us to spend brainlessly is through advertising. Advertisements are designed to be eye-catching and attention-grabbing, using bright colors and catchy slogans to draw us in. They often present products in a way that makes them seem essential or desirable, suggesting that we will be happier, more successful, or more attractive if we possess them. This kind of emotional appeal can be very effective, particularly if we are feeling vulnerable or insecure. However, it can also lead us to make impulsive decisions that we may later regret.

Another way that large corporations encourage brainless spending is by making it easy and convenient for us to buy their products. Online shopping, for example, has made it easier than ever to make purchases without leaving our homes. Many companies also offer free shipping or other incentives to encourage us to buy more. While this may be convenient, it also makes it easier to spend money without really thinking about it. We may add items to our online shopping cart without really considering whether we need them or how they fit into our budget.

A third way that large corporations encourage brainless spending is by using pricing strategies that make it difficult to compare the value of different products. For example, they may use deceptive pricing tactics that make it seem like we are getting a good deal, when in fact we are paying more than we should. They may also offer discounts or incentives for buying in bulk or for signing up for subscriptions, even if we don't actually need or want that much of a particular product.

Overall, it is clear that modern large corporations have a vested interest in encouraging brainless spending. However, this kind of consumption has many negative consequences, both for our personal financial well-being and for the health of our society as a whole. We must be vigilant in resisting these tactics and taking a more thoughtful approach when it comes to spending our hard-earned money. Only then can we truly take control of our financial futures and ensure that our decisions are based on our needs and values, rather than on the whims of corporate marketing departments.

The Psychology of Pretentious Spending

Pretentious spending refers to the act of spending money on items or experiences to project a certain image or social status, rather than for practical or functional reasons. Psychologically, pretentious spending is often rooted in the desire for validation, status, and social approval.

One of the main psychological factors driving pretentious spending is social identity theory. This theory posits that individuals feel a need to belong to a certain group, and that their self-esteem is highly dependent on their status within that group. In the context of pretentious spending, an individual may feel the need to purchase expensive items or experiences in order to gain acceptance and approval from their social group. By displaying their wealth and status through their purchases, they hope to solidify their position within the group and boost their self-esteem.

Another psychological factor at play in pretentious spending is conspicuous consumption. Coined by sociologist Thorstein Veblen, this theory suggests that individuals engage in conspicuous consumption as a way to signal their wealth and power to others. By purchasing luxury items or experiences, individuals communicate their social status and assert their dominance over others. In many cases, the act of pretentious spending is more about the perception others have of the spender, rather than the actual enjoyment or utility derived from the purchase.

Research has also shown that pretentious spending can be related to feelings of insecurity and low self-esteem. For instance, studies have found that individuals who feel a lack of control over their lives may engage in ostentatious spending as a way to gain a sense of control and power. Additionally, individuals who perceive themselves as less skilled or talented than others may use their wealth as a way to compensate for their perceived shortcomings.

Pretentious spending is a complex phenomenon that is driven by a variety of psychological factors. Whether it's the desire for social approval, the need for status and power, or feelings of insecurity, the act of pretentious spending is often more about psychological needs than practical ones. By understanding the psychology behind pretentious spending, we can gain insight into how our spending habits are influenced by our thoughts, feelings, and motivations.

Consumerism, Materialism is Good for the Economy, But not Good for Us!

Consumerism can be defined as a social and economic system in which the consumption of goods and services is highly valued, promoting economic growth and encouraging individuals to buy more and more. The idea that consumerism is good for the economy is highly debated, as it has both positive and negative effects on our society. While it is true that consumerism contributes to the growth of the economy, there are many negative consequences such as an increase in debt, pollution, and the erosion of social values.

One of the primary reasons why consumerism is good for the economy is that it contributes to economic growth. Consumer spending accounts for a large percentage of the Gross Domestic Product (GDP) in many countries, and as such, consumerism drives the economy forward. As people buy more goods and services, demand for these products rises, creating employment opportunities and driving innovation. This, in turn, leads to more job opportunities, more tax revenue for governments, and an overall increase in the standard of living.

However, the idea that consumerism is good for us is highly contentious. Consumerism has led to an increase in debt, as people continue to purchase items they cannot afford, relying heavily on credit cards and loans. This has resulted in a culture in which people are driven by the consumption of the newest and latest products without considering the long-term financial consequences. In addition, consumerism has contributed to environmental degradation, as people continue to consume products that contribute to carbon emissions, plastic pollution, and waste production. The environment suffers significantly as a result of the never-ending need for growth in the economy.

Consumerism has also had a profound impact on social values. People are becoming increasingly isolated from their communities, as they spend more time consuming goods and services, and less time interacting with others. The culture of consumerism has led many people to prioritize their own needs and desires over those of others, promoting greed, and selfishness.

Furthermore, the pressure to purchase and consume the latest products has a profound impact on self-esteem, as individuals feel that their worth is linked to the things they own.

While consumerism is a fundamental driving force behind economic growth, it comes with significant negative consequences. While it may be good for the economy, it is not good for us as individuals and as a society. It leads to increased debt, environmental degradation, and an erosion of social values. Therefore, it is essential to strike a balance between the benefits of consumerism and its negative consequences, promoting sustainable economic growth that takes into account the long-term effects of consumption.

Materialism is a philosophy that emphasizes the importance of material possessions and consumption. It is a driving force behind the modern economy, as it encourages people to constantly buy products, services, and experiences to boost economic growth. However, while materialism may be good for the economy, it is not necessarily good for us as individuals or as a society.

One of the main reasons why materialism is good for the economy is that it creates demand for goods and services. Businesses are motivated to create new products and services to appeal to consumers, who are constantly seeking to acquire more and better things. This creates jobs and drives economic growth, as businesses need employees to produce and market their goods, and consumers need income to purchase them.

However, while materialism may be good for businesses and economic growth, it has negative consequences for individuals and society as a whole. One of the most obvious examples of this is the environmental damage caused by constant consumption. As people buy and discard more and more products, landfills fill up, natural resources are depleted, and pollution increases. This can have serious consequences for the health and well-being of both people and the planet.

Another negative consequence of materialism is that it promotes a focus on superficial values, such as the pursuit of status and wealth, rather than on more meaningful values like love, compassion, and personal growth. This can lead to a sense of emptiness or dissatisfaction, as people try to fill the void in their lives with material possessions rather than with genuine connections and experiences.

Materialism can also contribute to inequality and social division. As people become more obsessed with acquiring wealth and status, they may be less likely to share resources or to work for the common good. This can lead to a breakdown in social cohesion, as people focus more on their own interests and less on the needs of others.

GOODBUY, THINGS!

While materialism may be good for the economy, it is not good for us as individuals or as a society. It promotes superficial values, damages the environment, and contributes to inequality and social division. Therefore, we need to find a better balance between economic growth and personal well-being, and to focus on creating a more sustainable and equitable future for all.

In our society today, it is often considered desirable to live a life of luxury and extravagance. The media incessantly portrays images of flashy cars, designer clothes, and lavish vacations, creating a skewed perception that wealth equals happiness. However, it is essential to remember that pretentious spending does not always make us happy.

Money itself, undoubtedly, cannot buy happiness. Studies have shown that beyond a certain threshold of income, more money does not improve our quality of life. The correlation between income and happiness is not very strong, and beyond a certain point, it becomes almost negligible. Money alone, therefore, cannot bring us true happiness.

Living a life of excess and pretentious spending often leads to overconsumption, which in turn leads to a feeling of emptiness and dissatisfaction. Constantly chasing after the latest trends and luxuries can create a culture of perpetual desire and dissatisfaction, making people feel that they are "missing out" on something if they don't have it. As a result, people tend to rely on material possessions to create a sense of happiness and self-worth, which ultimately leads to a shallow and unsustainable lifestyle.

Pretentious spending also creates an unhealthy focus on external validation. When we spend money on expensive, superficial things to impress others, we begin to rely on their approval for our happiness, leading to an insatiable need for external validation. Most times, such validation isn't forthcoming as people tend to value us for our character and not for our possessions. This realization of our superficiality and the realization that we have gotten so caught up in a culture of pretentious spending leaves us even more unfulfilled.

It is important to recognize that true happiness comes from within. Pursuing pretentious spending may provide momentary satisfaction, but it rarely sustains long-term happiness. Instead, it is essential to focus on building meaningful relationships, pursuing personal growth, and making choices that align with our values and passions. True happiness is found in purposeful living that emphasizes personal fulfillment, self-awareness and exploring our creativity, and not on materialistic pursuits.

Pretentious spending neither guarantees happiness nor long-term fulfillment. We should shift our focus from materialism to meaningful pursuits that give us space to focus on our mental wellbeing, relationships, and personal growth. Real happiness comes from within ourselves and will always be within our control rather than the superficial world we try to buy our way into.

Part Three: The Negative Psychological Effect of Too Much Materialism

The Battles Between Material Wealth and Spiritual Wealth

The concept of wealth has always been a central concern for human beings, as it refers to their access to resources and well-being. However, there has been a longstanding debate over the types of wealth that matter the most: material or spiritual. Both of these types of wealth have their own benefits and challenges, and the question of which is more important often comes down to personal beliefs and values.

Material wealth refers to any resources that can be used to satisfy human wants and needs. This includes money, property, and possessions such as cars, homes, and luxury goods. Material wealth is often valued for its ability to create comfort, happiness, and a sense of security. However, there are many drawbacks to excessive material wealth. It can lead to greed, selfishness, and a lack of empathy for those who are less fortunate. Additionally, material wealth is often fleeting, as it can be lost or destroyed at any time.

On the other hand, spiritual wealth refers to the intangible qualities that give meaning and purpose to life. This includes values such as love, compassion, gratitude, and humility. Spiritual wealth is often valued for its ability to create deeper connections and enrich human relationships. However, it can also be challenging to cultivate and maintain, as it requires individuals to constantly work on themselves and their relationships with others.

The battles between material and spiritual wealth are evident in many aspects of society. For example, in the business world, companies often prioritize profits over social responsibility and environmental sustainability. This emphasis on material wealth can lead to negative consequences for community members and the environment.

Similarly, in personal relationships, individuals may prioritize their material wealth over their spiritual well-being. This can lead to strained relationships and a lack of fulfillment in life. Conversely, those who prioritize their spiritual well-being often experience greater happiness and a sense of purpose, even if they may not have as much material wealth.

Ultimately, the battles between material wealth and spiritual wealth will continue to be a central concern for individuals and society as a whole. While both types of wealth have their own benefits and challenges, it is important to strive for a balance that promotes personal growth, fulfillment, and social responsibility. This may require a shift in societal values and a greater emphasis on holistic approaches to well-being.

Greed and Fear of Materialistic Life

Materialism can be motivated by strong emotions like greed and fear. It's easy to fall in love with the idea of having more and more things, but it's important to keep in mind that having too much materialism can have bad effects.

The excessive desire for possessions that is often motivated by greed and fear can be defined as materialism. Fear is the fear of not having enough, whereas greed is the desire for more and more possessions regardless of need or cost. At the point when these two feelings become interwoven, it can lead individuals to seek after realism more forcefully and unreasonably than needed.

People lose their ability to appreciate the simple pleasures of life when they become too focused on material possessions. It's possible that they'll become so preoccupied with accumulating more possessions that they forget to appreciate what they already have. A lack of financial security can also result from materialism. Financial stress and anxiety can result from individuals who become obsessed with accumulating more and more possessions.

Additionally, materialism may result in a distorted sense of one's own worth. People who become obsessed with their possessions may begin to believe that their worth is determined not by their achievements and qualities but rather by the things they own. Insecurity and feelings of inferiority can result from this belief.

It is essential to keep in mind that having possessions can be advantageous. Although having too many possessions isn't necessarily bad, it can have serious consequences. Taking a step back to appreciate what one already has and recognizing when greed and fear are driving one's pursuit of materialism are important. Possessions of material things can be a source of happiness, but it's important not to let them become the sole focus of one's life.

Part Four: Think Well Before You Buy Something

Things are Not Expensive. Just Check the Price of Wholesale Market, or Wholesale Websites

In today's world, it is easy to get carried away with buying things that we don't necessarily need. With the internet, we can easily purchase anything in a matter of minutes, without giving any thought to the cost. While it may seem that the things we buy are expensive, it is important to consider the marketing efforts that go into making us think so.

Marketing is a huge industry, and many businesses spend a lot of money on it. They use various techniques to make us think that their products are worth the cost. These techniques can include advertising, discounts, and other sales tactics. As a result, the price that we pay for the item is often inflated.

By doing a little research, we can actually find the same items at a much lower price. Many websites offer wholesale prices, which mean that we can get the same item at a much lower cost. It is also important to consider the quality of the item in question, as lower-quality items may not be worth the cost even if they are cheaper.

It is important to think well before buying anything, as our buying habits are often shaped by the marketing efforts of large enterprises. By taking the time to check out wholesale websites and compare prices, we can make sure that we are getting the best deal for our money. Doing this can save us money in the long run, and ensure that we are not paying more than we should for something.

Most Price You Pay Are the Costs of Rent, Sales Commisions, and Marketing Expenses

The sticker price on products habitually hides the genuine expense. It is not uncommon for the price of a product to be significantly higher than the costs involved in its production. This is because the price of a product frequently includes the costs of marketing, labor, rent, and the financial costs of the business.

Take for instance diamonds. While it is possible to mine and cut a diamond for very little money, the final product can cost thousands of dollars. This is because diamond companies have to pay for things like marketing and advertising, labor costs for cutting diamonds, rent for factories, and financial costs like taxes and overhead.

Gemstones, expensive cosmetics and perfumes, and high-end brands are all examples of this. Despite the fact that these items may be produced at a low cost, the production costs of marketing and labor frequently result in a significantly higher final price for the customer.

Because of this, it is essential to keep in mind that the cost of a product includes more than just the cost of production when making a purchase. It also includes the cost of labor and marketing, as well as rent and other financial expenses. This is why, despite having much lower manufacturing costs, some items may appear to be so expensive.

Throughout history, gemstones and diamonds have been viewed as symbols of power, love, and wealth. However, rather than their rarity, the price of these precious stones is determined by the successful marketing efforts of some previous businessmen.

Gemstones like rubies, emeralds, and sapphires have also benefited from successful marketing campaigns. At the turn of the 20th century, jewelers began to promote gemstones as symbols of power and wealth. Gemstones turned out to be very well known among the rich because of this promoting effort's prosperity. Because of this demand, the prices of gemstones went up, making them even more desirable.

Today, the success story of diamonds and gemstones is still driven by marketing efforts. Businesses continue to market diamonds and gemstones as symbols of wealth and luxury, maintaining their high prices. It is abundantly clear that a number of previous businessmen were largely to blame for the success of these precious stones and their ability to successfully generate market demand for them.

Part Five: How and Why to Reorganize Our Homes

Throw away Things We Don't Need

In this day and age, it can be detrimental to our mental and spiritual health to consume an excessive amount of anything. It is possible for things we no longer need or use to accumulate in our homes, resulting in an overwhelming sense of chaos and stress. It is vital to require the investment to go through our homes and give, reuse, or discard things that we needn't bother with. Doing this can be inconceivably valuable for our psychological wellness and otherworldly prosperity.

Clearing out our homes of clutter is one of the primary advantages of getting rid of things we no longer need. A sense of disarray and chaos caused by clutter can be extremely stressful and overwhelming. We can achieve a sense of calm and order in our homes by getting rid of unnecessary items. This can help us feel more at ease and relaxed.

Purging our homes can be good for our mental and spiritual well-being as well as our physical health. We are able to let go of the past and open ourselves up to new experiences when we get rid of things that have been holding us back. Getting rid of clutter can help us gain clarity, allowing us to concentrate on the things that are most important to us and strengthen our relationships with others and ourselves.

Additionally, getting rid of things we no longer require can be environmentally friendly. We are contributing to resource conservation and reducing waste by donating or recycling items. Because it can help us to feel connected to the world around us and to know that we are making positive contributions, this can also be beneficial for our mental and spiritual well-being.

In general, it is essential to take the time to sort through our belongings in our homes and either donate, recycle, or toss anything that no longer serves us. Doing this can assist with clearing the messiness and make a feeling of quiet and request that can be helpful for our emotional wellness and profound prosperity. It can likewise assist us with relinquishing the past and free ourselves up to new encounters, while additionally adding to the climate in a positive manner.

How Our Living Environment Affects Our Spiritual Well-being

Our living environment has a profound impact on our spiritual well-being, which is an essential component of our overall health and well-being. Understanding the connection between our living environment and spiritual health can assist us in creating a life that is both healthier and more balanced.

Its a well known fact that our actual climate can essentially affect our psychological and close to home state. However, our physical surroundings also have an impact on our spiritual well-being. Because it can affect our connection to our inner self, our higher power, and the outside world, our living space can have a direct impact on our spiritual health.

For instance, it can be challenging to attain the peace and stillness necessary for spiritual growth and development if our living environment is cluttered and chaotic. On the other hand, if the place where we live is calm and peaceful, it can help us connect with the stillness and inner peace that are necessary for spiritual development.

Our spiritual well-being can also be directly affected by how our living space is designed. We can become more mindful and connected to our spiritual side by living in a space that is designed to bring peace and balance to our lives. On the other hand, it can be difficult for us to focus on our spiritual path and connect with our inner self in a living space that is designed to be disorganized and chaotic.

Our spiritual well-being can also be impacted by the people we live with. The people we live with can either help or hinder our spiritual development. We can open up and explore our spiritual path if we live with people who are open to spiritual growth and exploration. On the other hand, it can be difficult for us to connect with our spiritual side if we live with people who are closed off to spiritual exploration.

Our living environment can also have a more subtle impact on our spiritual well-being. For instance, the colors in our living spaces can have an impact on our spiritual state as well as our emotional state. Colors can have a direct effect on how we feel, which can make us feel good or bad and have an impact on our spiritual well-being.

So, our living climate can straightforwardly affect our otherworldly prosperity. Taking the time to create a living space that encourages spiritual exploration and growth is essential. We may be able to strengthen our connections to our higher power, our inner self, and the outside world as a result of this.

Keeping your living space clean and organized can have a positive impact on your spiritual well-being. A cluttered and disorganized home can make it difficult to focus on spiritual activities, while an orderly environment can help create an atmosphere conducive to spiritual growth.

The physical environment has a direct effect on our mental and emotional states. Clutter and mess can be distracting and even overwhelming, making it difficult to focus on spiritual matters and practices. Conversely, a neat and organized environment can foster a sense of peace and mental clarity, making it easier to concentrate on spiritual activities such as prayer, meditation and spiritual reading.

In addition, a tidy home can help create a sense of harmony within the family. A cluttered house can be a source of stress, creating tension and discord among family members. On the other hand, having a well-ordered home can promote a sense of unity and togetherness in the household, helping to cultivate a spiritual atmosphere.

Keeping a clean and organized home can have a positive effect on our emotional well-being. Clutter can be a reminder of unfinished tasks and projects, leading to feelings of guilt and frustration. By contrast, having a clean and orderly home can lead to feelings of accomplishment and satisfaction, which can in turn foster a positive attitude and better emotional health.

A neat and organized home can help us to make the most of our time. Clutter can be a major time waster, as it can be difficult to concentrate on tasks when surrounded by mess. An orderly home, however, can help us to maximize our time, allowing us to more easily focus on spiritual matters.

Reorganizing our home in a clean and tidy manner can be highly beneficial to our spiritual well-being. An orderly home can help create an atmosphere conducive to spiritual growth, promote a sense of harmony in the family, lead to greater emotional well-being and help us to make the most of our time.

Memory Implication of Things and Memories - Wanted or Unwanted Memories

Memories can have a significant impact on our day-to-day lives. They can shape who we are, how we see the world, and even how we act and react to things in our lives. Both good and bad memories are inextricably linked to real places and things, and they can have a significant impact on our feelings, minds, and spirits.

Physical reminders of past events have been shown to have a powerful emotional impact, frequently bringing up memories or emotions that were previously forgotten, according to research. For example, a study by the University of California, Los Angeles found that just looking at a physical object can bring back a flood of feelings and memories from the past. So, it's not surprising that many of us have things or places that bring back memories of good and bad times, and getting rid of these things can be a powerful way to heal our minds, hearts, and emotions.

Self-care can include getting rid of things that bring back memories. It can help us feel like we have come to an end and free us from the burden of difficult memories. It also has the potential to give us a sense of control and autonomy, allowing us to construct a brand-new story about our lives. Getting rid of any physical reminders of a traumatic experience, for instance, can be a crucial step in the healing process for someone who has been through one.

Self-compassion can also be practiced by removing reminders of past events. We can cultivate a sense of safety and security by acknowledging and letting go of any negative emotions associated with these items. For people who are dealing with mental health issues like anxiety and depression, this can be especially important.

Naturally, it is essential to keep in mind that it may not always be possible or desirable to get rid of physical reminders of past events. For instance, it might not be possible to get rid of a family heirloom or something that has a lot of sentimental value. Still, taking a few moments to think about the memories associated with the object and practicing self-compassion can be helpful.

Our lives can be profoundly affected emotionally by physical reminders of past events. Eliminating a portion of these updates can be a strong method for recuperating our feelings, psyches, and spirits. We can move on with our lives if it gives us a sense of closure, control, and self-compassion.

The Perfect Arrangement of Home and Space

If you want to make your home a pleasant place to be, you need to arrange it in the best way possible. There are a few strategies that can assist you in creating the ideal atmosphere, whether you are starting from scratch or looking to improve an existing residence.

Start with the Furniture The first step toward a well-organized home is to buy new furniture. Choose items that look good and are useful at the same time. Ensure you measure the accessible space before you begin shopping. This will assist you in selecting the best type, size, and shape of furniture for the room.

Include a Focal Point A room's focal point is a key feature that draws attention to the space. This could be furniture, an artwork, or a fireplace, depending on the room's purpose. Make sure it stands out and sets the mood for the room, whichever it is.

Add Color A great way to make the environment feel good is to add color. A space can be brightened and important features brought to attention with bright accents. Try different color combinations until you find one that works best for you.

Include Greenery Adding greenery to a room is a simple way to give it life. Plant a few plants all over the room to give it a unique appearance and make it feel more peaceful.

Consider lighting Lighting is an essential component of any home arrangement. Always keep in mind how the room's atmosphere will be affected by the natural light. If you want your space to feel warm and inviting, add overhead lights and lamps.

It takes time and effort to organize your home in the most effective manner, but the results are well worth it. With the assistance of these con artists, you can create a charming climate that you will cherish for many years to come.

Simplicity and Minimalism

Because they have the potential to positively influence our spiritual well-being as well as our mental health, minimalism and simplicity are essential components of interior design. Living in a cluttered home can make you feel stressed and anxious, according to studies, whereas living in a clean, simple space can help you relax and feel at peace inside.

A chaotic and overwhelming home can result from clutter. It very well may be hard to zero in on the current second when encircled by such a lot of stuff. It can likewise make a sensation of being trapped before and the future, which can prompt sensations of gloom, tension, and stress.

On the other hand, a home that is minimalist and uncomplicated can be peaceful and calming. We can create a space that is free of distractions when we declutter our homes and concentrate on the essentials. Focusing on the here and now and paying attention to our emotions and thoughts might benefit from this.

A minimalist home can help us cultivate a sense of self-discipline as well as promote relaxation. It may be simpler for us to adhere to our routines and objectives when we are surrounded by fewer possessions. Because it can assist us in staying on track with our goals and having a sense of purpose, this can be beneficial to our mental health.

Lastly, a minimalist home can assist us in recognizing the beauty in our surroundings. We can become more aware of the beauty of our home and the world around us when we are surrounded by fewer possessions. We might be able to develop an appreciation for the here and now and the things we have thanks to this.

Arranging the interior design of our home using minimalism and simplicity is beneficial to both our mental and spiritual health. Relaxation, self-discipline, and appreciation of the beauty of the world around us can all benefit from it.

Neat and Tidy!

It should be everyone's goal to keep their home clean. A well-managed and well-organized home will result in a more upbeat and productive environment. You should make your dream home a clean one for the following reasons:

First and foremost, a tidy home will help you feel calm and relaxed. It's nice to come home after a long day at work to a place that is clean and clutter-free. It contributes to stress reduction and enhances tranquility.

Second, maintaining a clean home encourages a sense of responsibility. Everyone in the house is encouraged to take care of their belongings when everything is organized and in its proper place. Children will learn how important it is to take care of their belongings and clean their surroundings thanks to this.

Thirdly, keeping your house neat and tidy can help you save time. Things are easier to find and complete when everything is organized. This is especially helpful for families with multiple people and activities who are always on the go.

Last but not least, having a tidy home can help you save money. It is simpler to track what needs to be purchased and what can be reused when everything is organized. In the long run, this can help you save money by lowering the amount of money spent on unnecessary purchases.

Your ideal home ought to be clean and tidy. It promotes responsibility, promotes calm, and saves time and money at the same time. A more upbeat and productive work environment will result from each of these elements. Make your dream home today with organization!

Part Six: Do Things Really Make Us Happy? The True Costs of Luxury Items

The majority of people believe that luxury items come with high prices. However, what many of us aren't aware of is that luxury goods have much lower real manufacturing costs than the price tag suggests.

Take, for instance, a handbag from a posh brand. The materials used to make the bag may cost no more than $20 to produce on their own. However, its retail price may exceed $300 when it is placed on store shelves. This is due to the fact that luxury brands typically account for the price of R&D as well as their own markups and profit margins.

Luxury automobiles are the same. The German Centre for Automotive Research conducted a study that found that producing a luxury mid-range car typically costs around $20,000 on average. However, these automobiles have much higher starting prices, ranging from $50,000 to $100,000. This is because luxury car manufacturers have to pay for their own overhead as well as the costs associated with producing and marketing their vehicles.

The luxury watch industry is no exception. The expense of delivering an extravagance watch is assessed to be around $200, yet the retail cost might really depend on $1,000 or more. The watch's higher price tag is a result of the price of the materials used to make it and the cost of research and development.

A similar guideline applies to other extravagance things, for example, creator garments and shoes, gems, and, surprisingly, very good quality hardware. The item's manufacturing cost is significantly less than the retail price in each case.

Overall, it is evident that luxury brands produce luxury goods at very low costs and then sell them to us at very high prices. This is simply because the retail price includes the costs of research and development as well as their own overhead.

Are We Programmed to Release Dopamine When We Spend?

We are all aware of how satisfying it is to shop, particularly when we obtain what we truly desire. It's similar to feeling a surge of happiness or energy. However, what is it about spending money that gives us this impression?

As indicated by a new Stanford College study, dopamine might be at fault. The brain makes a hormone called dopamine that makes us feel happy and satisfied. When we accomplish something that makes us happy, dopamine is released, and this feeling makes us want to do the same thing over and over again.

This information has been used by advertisers to encourage customers to spend more. They create convincing advertisements that influence our brains to release dopamine and encourage us to make a purchase. Breaking this never-ending cycle of buying and spending can be difficult.

Given the state of affairs and the point at which we run out of money, are marketers programming our brains to release dopamine? The response is "yes." To get us to buy more of their products, marketers use our natural response to enjoyable activities.

But not everything is bad. If we are aware of the ways in which advertisers attempt to manipulate us, we can take control of our spending patterns. We can also control our spending and exercise self-control. We can break the cycle of spending and buying and make better financial decisions by doing this.

Our brains are ultimately programmed to respond to pleasure. With a little restraint, we can, however, break the pattern of buying and spending and make better financial decisions.

Do We Get the Same Dopamine When We Let Go of Useless?

The idea that our brains are programmed to release dopamine when we spend money has recently sparked a lot of debate. The power of advertising, which has been found to have a significant impact on consumer behavior, has been cited as the cause of this phenomenon.

Advertisers use this knowledge to convince us to spend money because they are aware of our natural inclination to be drawn to visuals and emotionally charged messages. Dopamine production has been found to rise in response to exposure to images of desirable products, according to research. As a result, it would appear that marketers are able to influence our minds into believing that making a purchase will result in happiness and contentment.

But if we learn to let go of materialism and stop relying on spending money to feel good, what will happen? Are we getting the same amount of dopamine as before?

The response is "yes." Our brains continue to produce dopamine even when we are able to concentrate on something else instead of material possessions, according to studies. This means that rather than relying on spending money to feel better, we can do things that make us happy, like hang out with friends, read a book, or go for a walk.

In general, it would appear that our brains are programmed to release dopamine when we spend money, but this does not imply that we must rely on material possessions to feel good. We can still get the same amount of dopamine without spending a penny by learning to concentrate on other activities that make us happy.

Part Seven: The Science of True Happiness
The Physiology of Happiness

Despite being one of the most sought-after feelings in life, happiness has been difficult to comprehend. The physiology of happiness, or the biological process by which humans experience happiness, has long fascinated scientists and researchers. In this article, we will look at how happiness is based in the body and how this knowledge can help us feel and keep joy in our lives.

Investigating the roles that hormones and neurotransmitters play in our emotional states is the first step in gaining an understanding of the physiological basis of happiness. Chemical messengers known as neurotransmitters carry signals between brain neurons. It is known that neurotransmitters like dopamine, serotonin, oxytocin, and endorphins are important for feeling happy. Dopamine, which is released whenever we experience pleasure or reward, is frequently referred to as the "happiness hormone." The neurotransmitter that is linked to feelings of contentment and well-being is serotonin. When we engage in activities that foster trust and connection, oxytocin—also known as the "love hormone"—is released. Endorphins can cause feelings of euphoria because they are released during physical activity.

One more significant figure understanding the physiology of bliss is the job of the endocannabinoid framework. Neuroreceptors and neurotransmitters make up the endocannabinoid system, which regulates mood, emotion, and motivation. Endocannabinoids are linked to feelings of happiness, contentment, and relaxation. It is known that they contribute to the pleasure experience.

Last but not least, it's important to think about how one's choices in life affect how happy they are. Our emotional states can be influenced by a variety of lifestyle factors, including physical activity, eating well, getting enough sleep, and social interaction. Serotonin and endorphin levels rise as a result of regular exercise, resulting in improved mood and well-being. Sleeping enough can help you sleep better and lessen your stress. A healthy diet can help us feel and have more energy.

Engaging in meaningful social activities has been shown to raise oxytocin levels and deepen relationships with others.

FAN XI YU

Knowing how happiness is based in the body can help us better understand how to find and keep joy in our lives. We can take steps to improve our overall well-being by comprehending the functions of hormones, the endocannabinoid system, and neurotransmitters, as well as the effects of our lifestyle choices.

Chemicals and Brainwave That Gives us Actual Happy Feelings

The human brain is a complex organ that produces numerous sensations and feelings. It might be one of its primary propensities to feel happy. A large number of natural synthetics delivered by our bodies add to this sensation. In this brief study, we will investigate the various chemicals that make us happy.

The most well-known chemical that makes people happy is serotonin. This neurotransmitter, which controls our mood, emotions, and social behavior, is produced in the brain. Anxiety, depression, and other mental health issues are thought to be controlled by it. Happiness is linked to higher levels of serotonin, whereas depression is linked to lower levels.

Another important chemical that makes people happy is dopamine. This neurotransmitter is in charge of the centers for pleasure and reward in the brain. We let go of our happiness when we do things that make us happy, like eating something delicious or having fun. When we accomplish a difficult task or goal, it is also released, which makes us feel good.

Another kind of chemical that makes you happy is endorphins. In response to stressful or painful situations, the brain releases endorphins. They can also naturally relieve pain and induce feelings of euphoria. Engaging in proactive activities like running or exercising can also result in the release of endorphins.

In the end, the chemical oxytocin is linked to trust and social connection. It is possible to experience feelings of fulfillment by spending time with people we care about. Helping with the administration of misery and anxiety is likewise thought.

There are a lot of biological chemicals in our bodies that can make us happy. It is anticipated that our long-term success will be influenced by endorphins, serotonin, dopamine, oxytocin, and other synthetic substances that are extremely significant neurotransmitters. We can all the more likely deal with our profound wellbeing and increment our degree of individual satisfaction by understanding the manufactured substances that satisfy us.

Compare the Hormone Levels: Exercise, Sex, Romance, Buying Things, Throwing Things Away

Throwing out of useless things from our home often ignores activities that can make us feel really happy. When there are many activities such as exercise, sex, romance and buy items that are said to be delighted, it may seem like a simple task - throwing old and unwanted items that will not do many of our emotional wells. However, the truth is that by throwing out useless things from our home can actually have a powerful positive effect on our hormone levels, which can lead to increased happiness.

When we exercise, our body releases endorphins that are good chemicals that make us feel happier and relaxed. Sex also releases endorphins, which often create an euphoric feeling. Romance also increases the level of endorphins and other hormones such as oxytocin, which can lead to a sense of communication and satisfaction. By buying things, we seem to be a sense of financial security and we can even give a short-term impetus for happiness.

However, when it comes to throwing useless things from our home, the effect of our hormone levels often overlooks. Throwing things we no longer use or need, can create a sense of relief and achievement as we will no longer bother the burden of clutter. This can increase dopamine, neurotransmitters associated with pleasure and reward. In addition, it can also reduce the amount of cortisol, the hormone associated with stress.

In general, the release of useless things from our home is a surprisingly effective activity that can really feel happy. This can help us reduce stress, increase dopamine levels and create a sense of achievement. So, next time looking for classes to make you happy, remember the simple task of throwing out useless things out of your home. You can just surprise you how it makes you feel.

The Purpose of Life

The Purpose of Life Life is an amazing journey with numerous ups and downs frequently. Appreciate Joy and Love Life. When you get caught up in worldly materialism, it's easy to forget the true purpose of life, which is to find love and happiness.

Living for material things is wrong. It might make you happy and content for a short period of time, but it won't make you happy and fulfilled for a long time. Feelings of emptiness, dissatisfaction, and unhappiness can result from materialism. It might prompt a feeling of disconnection from others and an absence of significant connections.

Real life motivation comes from realizing the value of pleasure and love. Being content is a state of happiness, and there are many different kinds of contentment. It could come from engaging pastimes and interests, fulfilling employment, or satisfying relationships with friends and family.

Another important aspect of life is love. It is a feeling that can be felt in a number of different settings, such as romantic relationships, relationships with loved ones, and even interactions with the natural world and environment. We experience a sense of connection and belonging thanks to the powerful emotion of love.

Our lives will be significantly more meaningful and satisfying if we concentrate on being happy and in love. We will be able to strengthen our interpersonal relationships, find meaning and purpose in our work and activities, and enjoy the little things in life every day. In addition, we will actually want to plan a life filled with significance, connection, and contentment.

Living for material things is wrong. In order to live a life that is both meaningful and satisfying, we ought to concentrate on experiencing love and happiness. When we do this, we will cultivate a more profound sense of direction and connection to our general surroundings.

- END -

Don't miss out!

Visit the website below and you can sign up to receive emails whenever Fan Xi Yu publishes a new book. There's no charge and no obligation.

https://books2read.com/r/B-A-BFSX-WALHC

BOOKS 2 READ

Connecting independent readers to independent writers.

Did you love *GoodBuy, Things!*? Then you should read *Optimism Is A Choice*[1] by Alison Atkinson!

[2]

The pandemic affects everyone, I know it is not easy to have lost someone dear to us, or our dream job, or our chance for education. There is a need to take better care of our spirit and mental health.And that is why I start writing this book.Prolonged turmoil in family lives, social lives and financial stress will have long term damage to our mental health. But if we address these issues timely, we still have chance to stop preventing to turn a season of mourning to a life time of grieve.I am lucky to be born as a millennial. So, like my peers, the society label me as such, and as usual, I rebel such labels as most millennials did.Until, when I met my fiancé, and spent time in knowing her family, I get to understand more about the silent generations and the baby-boomers. Then, by comparison, I realize that the 'characteristics' of millennials, as described by the internet, are somewhat authentic.In January 2020, when the Covid-19 pandemic begins, I predicted this event would come to an end within several months, like most

---

1. https://books2read.com/u/mYxvVd

2. https://books2read.com/u/mYxvVd

of the world's population did. These miscalculations did cost me a lot. Borders between nations were closed, and my life was stuck here for two years, without any option and ability to move forward, and financial stress starts to become overwhelmed.I never did imagine that one day I would become an author. It was the pandemic, this special situation that left me no choice but to pursuit a completely new career path, and thus, I chose to start writing books. The next question is, what topics to write?Hence, I start writing about self help books. I think humanity as a whole has experienced something unique in our time of history, and such traumatic experience will take up several years even after the pandemic has past, to recover.When I am writing this book, there is news that Pfizer is applying urgent approval for the Covid-19 pills, and the company has plans to overt the chemical formula of the drug for others to mass produce. That is a noble move. I hope this is it for the pandemic.In any time and situation, being optimistic is the best choice. We cannot control the outside world; all we have control is ourselves. The danger and chaos are real. But being optimistic or pessimistic, is simply a choice that we have free will to make. This is what I learnt from my fiancé, during the Covid-19 Pandemic.I hope this would help you to get through any tough situations.

About the Publisher

INPress International is a global publication organization that focuses on knowledges and topics where the traditional schooling system do not provide. Our Mission is to build a more humanistic, fair and peaceful future through our publication works.

www.ingramcontent.com/pod-product-compliance
Ingram Content Group UK Ltd.
Pitfield, Milton Keynes, MK11 3LW, UK
UKHW040703010525
5718UKWH00012B/168